Simple Guide to Java

Practical Guide

V. Telman

Copyright © 2024

Practical Guide

1. Introduction

Java is a high-level, class-based, object-oriented programming language designed to have as few implementation dependencies as possible. It is widely used for building web applications, mobile applications, and large-scale enterprise systems. Developed by Sun Microsystems and released in 1995, Java has consistently ranked among the most popular programming languages due to its versatility and performance.

Java is known for its portability; the motto "Write Once, Run Anywhere" (WORA) emphasizes how Java code can run on any device that has a Java Virtual Machine (JVM) installed, making it an ideal choice for cross-platform applications. In Java, the underlying principles of object-oriented programming (OOP) are deeply ingrained, which allows developers to create modular and maintainable code. Java supports several key features of OOP, including encapsulation, inheritance, and polymorphism.

Furthermore, Java has a rich set of libraries and frameworks that facilitate various programming tasks, from building graphical user interfaces (GUIs) to developing robust back-end services. Its extensive ecosystem includes popular frameworks such as Spring, Hibernate, and JavaFX, making it a powerful tool for developers across many domains.

The History of Java

The history of Java dates back to the early 1990s when James Gosling and a team of engineers at Sun Microsystems began the development of a programming language originally intended for interactive television. This project, known as the Green Project, was aimed at creating a language that could seamlessly run on various devices.

In 1995, Java was officially released to the public as a core component of Sun Microsystems' Java platform. The language quickly garnered attention due to its fundamental capabilities and "write once, run anywhere" philosophy. Java 1.0, the first official version, introduced the core features of Java, including its basic syntax, object-oriented capabilities, and a robust standard library.

Over the years, Java has gone through numerous updates and revisions, adding significant features and enhancements. Notable versions include:

- **Java 1.1** (1997): Introduced inner classes, JavaBeans, and the event model.

- **Java 2** (1998): Often referred to as Java 1.2, it introduced the Swing graphics API, Collections Framework, and improved performance.

- **Java 5** (2004): A major update that added generics, metadata, enhanced for-loop, and enumerated types, contributing to the language's robustness and type safety.

- **Java 8** (2014): Introduced lambda expressions, the Stream API, and the java.time package, enabling functional programming paradigms.

- **Java 11** (2018): The first Long-Term Support (LTS) version since Java 8, which simplified several aspects of the language and added numerous features.

With every subsequent version, Java has continued to innovate, maintaining its relevance in a rapidly evolving tech landscape. Oracle Corporation, which acquired Sun Microsystems in 2010, has since led Java's evolution, ensuring its ongoing development and support.

Why Learn Java?

Learning Java has numerous benefits that cater to both newcomers and experienced developers. Here are some key reasons to consider:

1. **Job Opportunities**: Java remains one of

the most sought-after programming languages in the job market. Many companies, especially those in finance, e-commerce, and large enterprise environments, rely on Java for their back-end systems.

2. **Cross-Platform Development**: The Java ecosystem supports various platforms and devices, making it an ideal choice for developers who want to build applications that can run on different operating systems.

3. **Object-Oriented Programming**: Java is fundamentally designed around OOP principles, which are crucial in modern software development. Understanding these concepts helps in writing maintainable and scalable code.

4. **Rich Ecosystem**: The extensive Java ecosystem includes powerful frameworks (like Spring and Hibernate) and libraries, which accelerate development time and provide solutions to common problems in app

development.

5. **Large Community Support**: Java has a vast and active developer community. Resources such as forums, Stack Overflow, and countless tutorials and documentation ensure that learners can easily find help and guidance.

6. **Performance and Scalability**: Machine-level optimizations and the Just-In-Time (JIT) compiler in the JVM allow Java applications to perform efficiently. These features contribute to Java's ability to scale and meet the demands of enterprise-level applications.

7. **Educational Value**: Java's clean syntax and structured programming approach makes it an excellent choice as a first programming language. Many computer science programs use Java to teach programming fundamentals, algorithms, and data structures.

Setting Up Your Development Environment

Before diving into Java programming, it's essential to set up your development environment properly. This includes installing the Java Development Kit (JDK) and configuring an Integrated Development Environment (IDE) to facilitate coding.

Installing Java Development Kit (JDK)

To start coding in Java, you need to install the Java Development Kit (JDK), which provides the necessary tools for developing Java applications, including a compiler and runtime environment.

1. **Download JDK**:

   - Visit the official Oracle website or the OpenJDK site (https://jdk.java.net/).

   - Make sure to download the version suited

for your operating system (Windows, macOS, or Linux).

2. **Install JDK**:

   - For Windows: Run the downloaded installer and follow the on-screen instructions. It's advisable to choose the option to set the Java environment variables automatically during installation.

   - For macOS: Open the downloaded .dmg file and drag the JDK package into your Applications folder.

   - For Linux: Follow the commands specific to your Linux distribution. You may need to use package managers like `apt` for Ubuntu or `yum` for Fedora.

3. **Verify Installation**:

   - Open a terminal or command prompt.

   - Type `java -version` and `javac -version`. If installed correctly, you should see the version number of the installed JDK.

Setting Up Integrated Development Environment (IDE)

While you can code in a simple text editor, using an IDE can significantly improve your development efficiency. IDEs provide features like code completion, debugging tools, and project management capabilities.

1. **Popular IDEs for Java**:

   - **Eclipse**: A powerful open-source IDE with a vast array of plugins.

   - **IntelliJ IDEA**: A widely-used IDE known for its intelligent coding assistance and ergonomics.

   - **NetBeans**: An open-source IDE supported by Oracle that is easy to use for Java development.

2. **Installing an IDE**:

- Download the installer from the official website of your chosen IDE.

- Follow the installation instructions for your operating system.

- After installation, configure the IDE to use the installed JDK by specifying the JDK path in the IDE's settings.

First Steps: Your First Java Program

Now that you have your development environment set up, it's time to write your very first Java program. This program will print "Hello, World!" to the console, serving as a simple introduction to Java syntax.

1. **Creating a New Project**:

   - Open your IDE and create a new Java project.

   - Specify the project name (e.g., HelloWorld) and save it in a designated directory.

2. **Writing the Java Code**:

   - In your new project, create a new Java class file named `HelloWorld.java`.

   - Use the following code:

```java
public class HelloWorld {
    public static void main(String[] args) {
        System.out.println("Hello, World!");
    }
}
```

Here's a breakdown of the code:

   - `public class HelloWorld` defines a class named `HelloWorld`.

   - The `main` method serves as the entry point of any Java application. It takes an array of String arguments.

   - `System.out.println("Hello, World!");` outputs the string to the console.

3. **Running the Program**:

   - In your IDE, find the option to run the Java application (commonly represented by a green play icon).

   - Upon running the program, you should see the text "Hello, World!" printed in the console.

4. **Understanding the Code**:

   - This minimal Java program demonstrates the basic structure of a Java application.

   - As you advance in Java programming, you will encounter classes, fields, methods, and various syntax elements regularly.

Java is a powerful and versatile programming language that has stood the test of time. With a rich history, a plethora of features, and extensive community support, learning Java opens many doors for aspiring and experienced developers alike. By setting up the appropriate development environment and writing your first program, you've taken the first steps into the exciting world of Java programming. As you continue to explore Java, you will discover its capabilities and the vast opportunities it offers in software development, web applications, mobile apps, and beyond. The journey may seem overwhelming at first, but with consistent practice and exploration, you'll find yourself mastering Java and becoming a successful developer in no time.

2.Java Basics

Java is a widely-used programming language that is known for its simplicity, portability, and robustness. Whether you're a seasoned developer or an aspiring programmer, understanding the basics of Java is crucial for building efficient applications. This article will cover the core concepts of Java, including variables, data types, operators, control flow statements, and exception handling, providing examples for clarity.

Understanding Variables and Data Types

What is a Variable?

A variable in Java is a container that holds data temporarily. It is a named memory location that can store different types of data. Before using a variable, you must define its data type, which determines what kind of data it can hold.

Data Types in Java

Java has two categories of data types:

1. **Primitive Data Types**: These are the basic types provided by Java. They are not objects and hold data directly in their memory location.

    - `int`: For integers (e.g., `int age = 25;`)

    - `double`: For floating-point numbers (e.g., `double salary = 2500.50;`)

    - `boolean`: For true/false values (e.g., `boolean isJavaFun = true;`)

    - `char`: For single characters (e.g., `char grade = 'A';`)

    - `byte`: For 8-bit signed integers, ranges from -128 to 127.

    - `short`: For 16-bit signed integers, ranges from -32,768 to 32,767.

    - `long`: For 64-bit signed integers, can store large numbers.

- `float`: For single-precision floating-point numbers, used when needing fractional points with less precision than `double`.

2. **Reference Data Types**: These are non-primitive data types, and they reference objects or arrays.

   - Strings (e.g., `String name = "John";`)
   - Arrays (e.g., `int[] numbers = {1, 2, 3, 4};`)
   - Classes and Interfaces

Example of Variable Declaration

```java
public class VariablesExample {
    public static void main(String[] args) {
        // Primitive Data Types
        int age = 25;
        double height = 5.9;
```

```java
        boolean isMarried = false;
        char initial = 'J';

        // Reference Data Type
        String name = "Alice";

        System.out.println("Name: " + name);
        System.out.println("Age: " + age);
        System.out.println("Height: " + height);
        System.out.println("Married: " + isMarried);
        System.out.println("Initial: " + initial);
    }
}
```

Operators in Java

Operators are special symbols in Java that perform specific operations on variables and values. Java provides various types of operators, including:

1. **Arithmetic Operators**: Used for mathematical calculations.

- `+` (addition)

- `-` (subtraction)

- `*` (multiplication)

- `/` (division)

- `%` (modulus)

Example:

```java
int a = 10;
int b = 20;
int sum = a + b; // sum = 30
```

2. **Relational Operators**: Used for comparing two values.

- `==` (equal to)
- `!=` (not equal to)
- `>` (greater than)
- `<` (less than)
- `>=` (greater than or equal to)
- `<=` (less than or equal to)

Example:

```java
if (a > b) {
    System.out.println("A is greater than B");
} else {
    System.out.println("A is not greater than B");
}
```

3. **Logical Operators**: Used to combine multiple conditions.

- `&&` (logical AND)

- `||` (logical OR)

- `!` (logical NOT)

Example:

```java
boolean condition1 = true;
boolean condition2 = false;

if (condition1 && condition2) {
    System.out.println("Both conditions are true");
} else {
    System.out.println("At least one condition is false");
}
```

4. **Assignment Operators**: Used to assign values to variables.

- `=` (simple assignment)
- `+=` (addition assignment)
- `-=` (subtraction assignment)
- `*=` (multiplication assignment)
- `/=` (division assignment)

Example:
```java
int x = 10;
x += 5; // x = 15
```

Control Flow Statements

Control flow statements enable decision-making in your Java programs, allowing you to execute different code paths based on conditions. There are various control flow statements in Java:

1. **If Statement**

The `if` statement evaluates a boolean condition and executes a block of code if the condition is true.

Example:

```java
int number = 10;

if (number < 0) {
    System.out.println("Number is negative");
} else if (number == 0) {
    System.out.println("Number is zero");
} else {
```

```
    System.out.println("Number is positive");
}
```

2. **Switch Statement**

The `switch` statement allows you to select one of many code blocks to execute based on the value of an expression.

Example:
```java
char grade = 'B';

switch (grade) {
    case 'A':
        System.out.println("Excellent");
        break;
    case 'B':
```

```
    System.out.println("Well done");
        break;
   case 'C':
       System.out.println("Good");
       break;
   case 'D':
       System.out.println("You passed");
       break;
   case 'F':
       System.out.println("Better luck next time");
       break;
   default:
       System.out.println("Invalid grade");
}
```

3. **Loops**

Loops allow you to execute a block of code repeatedly based on a condition.

For Loop:

This loop executes a block of code a specific number of times.

Example:

```java
for (int i = 0; i < 5; i++) {
    System.out.println("Iteration: " + i);
}
```

While Loop:

This loop continues executing as long as a specified condition is true.

Example:

```java
int j = 0;
while (j < 5) {
    System.out.println("Iteration: " + j);
    j++;
}
```

Do-While Loop:

Similar to the `while` loop, but it guarantees at least one execution of the code block.

Example:
```java
int k = 0;
do {
    System.out.println("Iteration: " + k);
    k++;
```

```
} while (k < 5);
```

Exception Handling

In Java, an exception is an unexpected event that occurs during the execution of a program, disrupting its normal flow. Exception handling is a mechanism that allows you to handle runtime errors in a controlled manner.

Try-Catch Block

The `try-catch` block is used to catch exceptions and handle them gracefully instead of terminating the program.

Example:

```java
public class ExceptionHandlingExample {
```

```java
public static void main(String[] args) {
    int[] numbers = {1, 2, 3};

    try {
        System.out.println(numbers[3]); // This will throw an ArrayIndexOutOfBoundsException
    } catch (ArrayIndexOutOfBoundsException e) {
        System.out.println("Caught an exception: " + e.getMessage());
    }

    System.out.println("Program continues...");
}
}
```

Finally Block

The `finally` block always executes after the `try-catch` block, regardless of whether an exception was thrown or caught. It is typically used for cleanup code, such as closing files or releasing resources.

Example:

```java
public class FinallyBlockExample {
    public static void main(String[] args) {
        try {
            int result = 10 / 0; // This will throw an ArithmeticException
        } catch (ArithmeticException e) {
            System.out.println("Caught an exception: " + e.getMessage());
        } finally {
            System.out.println("This block always executes.");
```

        }
    }
}
```


#### Throwing Exceptions

You can also throw exceptions using the `throw` statement. This is useful for creating your own custom exceptions.

**Example**:
```java
public class ThrowExceptionExample {
    public static void checkAge(int age) {
        if (age < 18) {
            throw new IllegalArgumentException("Not eligible to vote");

```java
        } else {
            System.out.println("Eligible to vote");
        }
    }

    public static void main(String[] args) {
        try {
            checkAge(16);
        } catch (IllegalArgumentException e) {
            System.out.println("Caught an exception: " + e.getMessage());
        }
    }
}
```

Understanding the basics of Java, including variables, data types, operators, control flow statements, and exception handling is fundamental for anyone looking to develop applications in Java. These concepts lay the groundwork for making your code more efficient, reliable, and flexible. As you move forward, you can delve deeper into advanced topics, libraries, and frameworks, all built upon these foundational principles.

By mastering these basics, you enhance your programming skills and prepare yourself for more complex challenges in your journey as a Java developer.

3. Object-Oriented Programming in Java

Object-Oriented Programming (OOP) is a programming paradigm that uses "objects" to design applications and computer programs. It bundles data (attributes) and methods (functions) that operate on the data into a single unit called a class. Java is a widely-used object-oriented programming language that provides several features to facilitate OOP.

This article will delve into the core concepts of OOP in Java, including classes and objects, inheritance and polymorphism, encapsulation and abstraction, as well as interfaces and abstract classes. Each of these concepts will be illustrated with examples to enhance comprehension.

Classes and Objects

Classes

A class in Java serves as a blueprint for creating objects. It defines attributes (fields) and methods that the objects created from the class will have. A class can contain constructors, fields, and methods.

Example of a Class:

```java
public class Car {
    // Attributes
    private String make;
    private String model;
    private int year;

    // Constructor
```

```java
    public Car(String make, String model, int year) {
        this.make = make;
        this.model = model;
        this.year = year;
    }


    // Methods
    public void displayDetails() {
        System.out.println("Car Make: " + make);
        System.out.println("Car Model: " + model);
        System.out.println("Car Year: " + year);
    }
}
```

Objects

An object is an instance of a class. When a class is defined, no memory is allocated for the class itself. Memory is allocated only when an object of the class is created. You can create multiple objects from the same class, each with its own attributes.

Example of Creating Objects:

```java
public class Main {
    public static void main(String[] args) {
        // Creating objects of Car class
        Car car1 = new Car("Toyota", "Corolla", 2022);
        Car car2 = new Car("Honda", "Civic", 2023);
```

```
        // Displaying details of the objects
        car1.displayDetails();
        car2.displayDetails();
    }
}
```

Output:

```
Car Make: Toyota
Car Model: Corolla
Car Year: 2022
Car Make: Honda
Car Model: Civic
Car Year: 2023
```

Inheritance and Polymorphism

Inheritance

Inheritance is a mechanism in OOP that allows a new class to inherit the properties and methods of an existing class. The class that inherits is called the child (or subclass), and the class being inherited from is called the parent (or superclass).

Example of Inheritance:

```java
// Superclass
public class Vehicle {
    protected String type;

    public Vehicle(String type) {
        this.type = type;
```

```java
    }

    public void displayType() {
        System.out.println("Vehicle Type: " + type);
    }
}

// Subclass
public class Bike extends Vehicle {
    private String brand;

    public Bike(String brand) {
        super("Bike"); // Calling the constructor of the superclass
        this.brand = brand;
    }

    public void displayDetails() {
```

```
        displayType();
        System.out.println("Bike Brand: " + brand);
    }
}
```

Polymorphism

Polymorphism allows methods to do different things based on the object that it is acting upon. There are two types of polymorphism in Java:

1. **Compile-time polymorphism (method overloading)**

2. **Runtime polymorphism (method overriding)**

Example of Method Overloading (Compile-time Polymorphism):

```java
public class MathUtils {
    public int add(int a, int b) {
        return a + b;
    }

    public double add(double a, double b) {
        return a + b;
    }
}
```

Example of Method Overriding (Runtime Polymorphism):

```java
```

```java
// Superclass
public class Animal {
    public void sound() {
        System.out.println("Animal makes a sound");
    }
}


// Subclass
public class Dog extends Animal {
    @Override
    public void sound() {
        System.out.println("Dog barks");
    }
}


// Subclass
public class Cat extends Animal {
```

```java
    @Override
    public void sound() {
        System.out.println("Cat meows");
    }
}
```

Example of Using Polymorphism:

```java
public class Main {
    public static void main(String[] args) {
        Animal myAnimal; // Declare an animal reference variable
        myAnimal = new Dog(); // Instantiate Dog
        myAnimal.sound(); // Outputs: Dog barks
```

```
        myAnimal = new Cat(); // Instantiate Cat

        myAnimal.sound(); // Outputs: Cat meows

    }
}
```

Encapsulation and Abstraction

Encapsulation

Encapsulation is the concept of wrapping data (variables) and methods (functions) together into a single unit, typically using classes. It restricts direct access to some components, which can enhance security and make the code more manageable.

Example of Encapsulation:

```java
public class BankAccount {
    private double balance; // Private variable

    public BankAccount(double initialBalance) {
        this.balance = initialBalance;
    }

    // Method to deposit money
    public void deposit(double amount) {
        if (amount > 0) {
            balance += amount;
        }
    }

    // Method to withdraw money
    public void withdraw(double amount) {
```

```java
        if (amount > 0 && amount <= balance) {
            balance -= amount;
        }
    }

    // Method to get the balance
    public double getBalance() {
        return balance;
    }
}


public class Main {
    public static void main(String[] args) {
        BankAccount account = new BankAccount(1000.00);
        account.deposit(500.00);
        account.withdraw(200.00);
        System.out.println("Current Balance: $" + account.getBalance()); // Outputs: Current
```

Balance: $1300.0

    }
}
```

### Abstraction

Abstraction is the concept of hiding the complex implementation details and showing only the essential features of an object. It can be achieved in Java using abstract classes and interfaces.

**Example of Abstraction with Abstract Class:**

```java
abstract class Shape { // Abstract class
    abstract void draw(); // Abstract method
}

```java
class Circle extends Shape {
    void draw() {
        System.out.println("Drawing a Circle");
    }
}

class Rectangle extends Shape {
    void draw() {
        System.out.println("Drawing a Rectangle");
    }
}

// Using the abstract class
public class Main {
    public static void main(String[] args) {
        Shape circle = new Circle();
```

```
        Shape rectangle = new Rectangle();


    circle.draw(); // Outputs: Drawing a Circle
    rectangle.draw(); // Outputs: Drawing a Rectangle
    }
}
```

Interfaces and Abstract Classes

Interfaces

An interface is a reference type in Java that is similar to a class but can only contain abstract methods, static methods, and final variables. Interfaces can be used to achieve abstraction and multiple inheritance.

An interface defines what a class can do, but not how it does it. A class that implements an interface must implement all of its methods.

Example of an Interface:

```java
interface Animal {
    void sound(); // Abstract method
    void eat();   // Abstract method
}

class Dog implements Animal {
    public void sound() {
        System.out.println("Dog barks");
    }

    public void eat() {
        System.out.println("Dog eats");
```

```java
        }
    }

    class Cat implements Animal {
        public void sound() {
            System.out.println("Cat meows");
        }

        public void eat() {
            System.out.println("Cat eats");
        }
    }

    // Using the interface
    public class Main {
        public static void main(String[] args) {
            Animal dog = new Dog();
            Animal cat = new Cat();
```

```
        dog.sound(); // Outputs: Dog barks
        cat.sound(); // Outputs: Cat meows
    }
}
```

Abstract Classes vs Interfaces

- **Abstract Classes:**

  - Can have methods with implementation (concrete methods).

  - Can have instance variables.

  - Can have constructors.

  - A class can only extend one abstract class.

- **Interfaces:**

  - Cannot have concrete methods (before Java 8), but can have default and static methods since Java 8.

- Cannot have instance variables (only static final variables).

- A class can implement multiple interfaces.

Example of an Abstract Class vs Interface:

```java
abstract class Vehicle {
    abstract void displayType();
}


interface Engine {
    void startEngine();
}


class Car extends Vehicle implements Engine {
```

```java
    public void displayType() {
        System.out.println("This is a Car");
    }

    public void startEngine() {
        System.out.println("Car engine started");
    }
}

// Using the abstract class and interface
public class Main {
    public static void main(String[] args) {
        Car car = new Car();
        car.displayType(); // Outputs: This is a Car
        car.startEngine(); // Outputs: Car engine started
    }
}
```

Object-Oriented Programming is a powerful paradigm that enables developers to build modular, reusable, and organized code. Understanding the principles of classes and objects, inheritance and polymorphism, encapsulation and abstraction, as well as interfaces and abstract classes is crucial for mastering Java and efficiently designing software applications that are robust and maintainable.

The examples provided in this article aim to give a comprehensive overview of essential OOP concepts in Java alongside practical implementations. Mastery of these concepts will greatly enhance your programming skills and empower you, as a developer, to create more efficient and scalable applications.

4. Java Collections Framework

The Java Collections Framework (JCF) is a unified architecture for representing and manipulating collections of objects in Java. It provides a set of interfaces, implementations, and algorithms for managing groups of objects efficiently. Collections can be thought of as containers that hold data, making it easier to work with related items. JCF is particularly useful for handling large amounts of data, facilitating various functionalities such as searching, sorting, and manipulation of groups.

The main benefits of using the Java Collections Framework include:

1. **Easy Maneuverability**: Collections provide a standard way to handle data, making it simpler to understand and manage more extensive data structures.

2. **Flexibility and Reusability**: JCF allows developers to switch between different data

structures without changing the fundamentally dependent code.

3. **Optimized for Performance**: JCF includes various algorithms optimized for performance, helping developers write efficient code with minimal overhead.

4. **Interoperability**: Compatible across various Java applications, ensuring components can work together smoothly.

The primary interfaces in JCF include **Collection**, **List**, **Set**, **Map**, among others, which help categorize the different types of data structures available.

Lists, Sets, and Maps

1. Lists

A List is an ordered collection (also known as a sequence) that allows duplicates. Lists can store elements in a specific order and can be accessed by their position (index). The most commonly used classes for implementing the List interface are **ArrayList**, **LinkedList**, and **Vector**.

Example of List with ArrayList

```java
import java.util.ArrayList;
import java.util.List;

public class ListExample {
    public static void main(String[] args) {
        List<String> fruits = new ArrayList<>();

        // Adding elements
        fruits.add("Apple");
        fruits.add("Banana");
        fruits.add("Orange");
```

```java
        fruits.add("Mango");

        // Add duplicate
        fruits.add("Apple");

        // Accessing elements
        System.out.println("Fruits list: " + fruits);

        // Access by index
        System.out.println("First fruit: " + fruits.get(0));

        // Removing an element
        fruits.remove("Banana");
        System.out.println("After removal: " + fruits);

        // Iterating over a list
        for (String fruit : fruits) {
```

```
            System.out.println("Fruit: " + fruit);
        }
    }
}
```

2. Sets

A Set is a collection that does not allow duplicates; it models the mathematical set abstraction. It is an unordered collection, meaning that the elements are not stored in a specific sequence. Commonly used Set implementations include **HashSet**, **LinkedHashSet**, and **TreeSet**.

Example of Set with HashSet

```java
import java.util.HashSet;
```

```java
import java.util.Set;

public class SetExample {
    public static void main(String[] args) {
        Set<Integer> numbers = new HashSet<>();

        // Adding elements
        numbers.add(10);
        numbers.add(20);
        numbers.add(30);
        numbers.add(20); // Duplicate, will not be added

        System.out.println("Numbers set: " + numbers);

        // Iterating over a set
        for (Integer number : numbers) {
```

```
            System.out.println("Number: " + number);
        }
    }
}
```

3. Maps

A Map is an object that maps keys to values, with each key being unique. Maps are not considered collections, but they are part of the Java Collections Framework. Common Map implementations include **HashMap**, **LinkedHashMap**, and **TreeMap**.

Example of Map with HashMap

```java
import java.util.HashMap;
```

```java
import java.util.Map;

public class MapExample {
    public static void main(String[] args) {
        Map<String, Integer> studentGrades = new HashMap<>();

        // Adding elements
        studentGrades.put("Alice", 90);
        studentGrades.put("Bob", 85);
        studentGrades.put("Charlie", 88);

        // Duplicate key (value will be overwritten)
        studentGrades.put("Alice", 95);

        System.out.println("Student Grades: " + studentGrades);
```

```
        // Accessing a value
    System.out.println("Alice's grade: " + studentGrades.get("Alice"));

    // Iterating over a map
    for (Map.Entry<String, Integer> entry : studentGrades.entrySet()) {
        System.out.println(entry.getKey() + ": " + entry.getValue());
    }
  }
}
```

Iterators and Enhanced For Loop

Iterators

An Iterator is an object that enables traversing

a collection sequentially without exposing the underlying details of the collection. It provides methods such as `hasNext()`, `next()`, and `remove()` to facilitate safe traversal and manipulation.

Example using Iterator with List

```java
import java.util.ArrayList;
import java.util.Iterator;
import java.util.List;

public class IteratorExample {
    public static void main(String[] args) {
        List<String> colors = new ArrayList<>();
        colors.add("Red");
        colors.add("Green");
        colors.add("Blue");
```

```java
        // Using iterator
        Iterator<String> iterator = colors.iterator();
        while (iterator.hasNext()) {
            String color = iterator.next();
            System.out.println("Color: " + color);
            // Remove green
            if (color.equals("Green")) {
                iterator.remove();
            }
        }


        System.out.println("Colors after removal: " + colors);
    }
}
```

Enhanced For Loop

The enhanced for loop, also known as the "for-each" loop, allows iterating over arrays and collections without needing an explicit iterator or index.

Example of Enhanced For Loop

```java
import java.util.ArrayList;
import java.util.List;

public class EnhancedForLoopExample {
    public static void main(String[] args) {
        List<String> countries = new ArrayList<>();
        countries.add("USA");
        countries.add("Canada");
```

```
        countries.add("Mexico");

        // Using enhanced for loop
        for (String country : countries) {
            System.out.println("Country: " + country);
        }
    }
}
```

Comparison and Sorting of Collections

Java provides the `Comparable` and `Comparator` interfaces for sorting collections.

Comparable Interface

The `Comparable` interface is used for natural ordering of objects. Classes implementing this interface need to override the `compareTo()` method.

Example of Comparable

```java
import java.util.ArrayList;
import java.util.Collections;
import java.util.List;

class Student implements Comparable<Student> {
    String name;
    int age;

    Student(String name, int age) {
        this.name = name;
```

```java
        this.age = age;
    }

    @Override
    public int compareTo(Student other) {
        return this.age - other.age; // Sort by age
    }

    @Override
    public String toString() {
        return name + ": " + age;
    }
}

public class ComparableExample {
    public static void main(String[] args) {
        List<Student> students = new ArrayList<>();
```

```
        students.add(new Student("Alice", 22));
        students.add(new Student("Bob", 20));
        students.add(new Student("Charlie", 21));

        Collections.sort(students); // Sorting using compareTo method
        System.out.println("Sorted Students: " + students);
    }
}
```

Comparator Interface

The `Comparator` interface can be used when a custom order is required. Classes implementing `Comparator` must override the `compare()` method.

Example of Comparator

```java
import java.util.ArrayList;
import java.util.Collections;
import java.util.Comparator;
import java.util.List;

class Employee {
    String name;
    double salary;

    Employee(String name, double salary) {
        this.name = name;
        this.salary = salary;
    }

    @Override
```

```java
    public String toString() {
        return name + ": " + salary;
    }
}


public class ComparatorExample {
    public static void main(String[] args) {
        List<Employee> employees = new ArrayList<>();
        employees.add(new Employee("Alice", 60000));
        employees.add(new Employee("Bob", 75000));
        employees.add(new Employee("Charlie", 50000));

        // Sorting by salary using a Comparator
        Collections.sort(employees, new Comparator<Employee>() {
            @Override
```

```java
        public int compare(Employee e1, Employee e2) {
            return Double.compare(e1.salary, e2.salary); // Sort by salary
        }
    });

    System.out.println("Sorted Employees: " + employees);
    }
}
```

The Java Collections Framework is a powerful and essential aspect of Java programming, allowing developers to perform complex data manipulation with ease. By understanding the concepts of Lists, Sets, Maps, Iterators, and Sorting Mechanisms, one can handle collections in an efficient, organized, and intuitive manner.

With an array of implementations to choose from, software developers can leverage JCF's capabilities to ensure their applications manage data effectively, whether dealing with simple collections or complex data interactions. Through thoughtful design and programming practices, Java Collections help maintain the integrity and performance of applications, making them indispensable for Java development.

5. Working with Java Streams

Java Streams are a powerful feature introduced in Java 8 that allows developers to process sequences of elements in a functional style. They provide a higher-level abstraction over collections and allow for a more concise and readable way to manipulate data. In this guide, we'll explore Streams in Java, starting from their introduction to various operations like filtering, mapping, reducing, and collecting data from streams.

Introduction to Streams

Streams represent a sequence of elements and provide a functional approach to process those elements. They do not store data; they simply convey the data from a source such as a collection, array, or I/O channel. A key aspect of streams is that they allow for functional-style programming, enabling developers to write code that is more intuitive and easier to understand.

Characteristics of Streams

1. **No storage**: Streams do not store elements; they only provide a view of data.

2. **Functional in nature**: Streams support functional programming, enabling operations like filtering, mapping, and reducing.

3. **Laziness-seeking**: Most stream operations are lazy, which means that computation is not performed until the result is actually needed. This can improve performance.

4. **Possibly unbounded**: While most streams are based on finite collections, it is possible to work with infinite streams.

5. **Consumption**: A stream is consumed once it has been operated on; they cannot be reused.

Creating Streams

A stream can be created from various data sources:

- From a collection (e.g., List, Set)

- From an array

- From I/O channels (files, sockets)

- From generator functions (e.g., `Stream.iterate()`)

Here are a few examples of creating streams:

```java
import java.util.Arrays;

import java.util.List;

import java.util.stream.Stream;

// Creating a Stream from a collection

List<String> names = Arrays.asList("Alice",
```

```
"Bob", "Charlie");

Stream<String> nameStream = names.stream();


// Creating a Stream from an array

String[] nameArray = {"David", "Eve", "Frank"};

Stream<String> arrayStream = Arrays.stream(nameArray);


// Creating an infinite Stream

Stream<Integer> infiniteStream = Stream.iterate(0, n -> n + 1).limit(10);
```
```

## Stream Operations: Filtering, Mapping, and Reducing

### Filtering
```

Filtering is a stream operation that allows for removing elements from a stream based on a predicate. The `filter` method is used for this purpose.

Example of filtering:

```java
import java.util.Arrays;
import java.util.List;
import java.util.stream.Collectors;

public class FilterExample {
    public static void main(String[] args) {
        List<String> names = Arrays.asList("Alice", "Bob", "Charlie", "David", "Eve");

        // Filtering names that start with 'A' or 'D'
        List<String> filteredNames =
```

```
names.stream()
        .filter(name -> name.startsWith("A") || name.startsWith("D"))
        .collect(Collectors.toList());

        System.out.println(filteredNames); // Output: [Alice, David]
    }
}
```

Mapping

Mapping transforms each element in a stream to another form. The `map` method is used for this transformation.

Example of mapping:

```java
import java.util.Arrays;
import java.util.List;
import java.util.stream.Collectors;

public class MapExample {
    public static void main(String[] args) {
        List<String> names = Arrays.asList("Alice", "Bob", "Charlie");

        // Mapping names to their lengths
        List<Integer> nameLengths = names.stream()
                                        .map(String::length)
                                        .collect(Collectors.toList());

        System.out.println(nameLengths); // Output: [5, 3, 7]
```

    }
}
```

### Reducing

Reducing is a terminal operation that aggregates the elements of a stream into a single result. The `reduce` method is typically used for this purpose.

Example of reducing:

```java
import java.util.Arrays;
import java.util.List;

public class ReduceExample {
    public static void main(String[] args) {

```java
        List<Integer> numbers = Arrays.asList(1, 2, 3, 4, 5);

        // Reducing to sum the numbers
        int sum = numbers.stream()
                .reduce(0, Integer::sum); // 0 is the identity value

        System.out.println(sum); // Output: 15
    }
}
```

Collecting Data from Streams

Collecting data from streams is a crucial aspect that allows the results of stream operations to be gathered into collections or other forms. In Java, the `collect` method is often employed for this purpose.

Using Collectors

The `Collectors` utility class provides several convenient static methods for collecting data. For example, you can collect elements into a list, set, or map.

Collecting to a List

```java
import java.util.Arrays;
import java.util.List;
import java.util.stream.Collectors;

public class CollectToListExample {
    public static void main(String[] args) {
        List<String> names = Arrays.asList("Alice", "Bob", "Charlie", "David", "Eve");
```

```
// Collecting names that contain the letter 'a' into a List
        List<String> collectedNames = names.stream()
                            .filter(name -> name.contains("a"))
                            .collect(Collectors.toList());

        System.out.println(collectedNames); // Output: [Alice, Charlie, David]
    }
}
```

Collecting to a Set

You can also collect stream elements into a set to avoid duplicates:

```java
import java.util.Arrays;
import java.util.List;
import java.util.Set;
import java.util.stream.Collectors;

public class CollectToSetExample {
    public static void main(String[] args) {
        List<String> names = Arrays.asList("Alice", "Bob", "Charlie", "David", "Eve", "Alice");

        // Collecting names into a Set
        Set<String> collectedNames = names.stream()

        .collect(Collectors.toSet());

        System.out.println(collectedNames); // Output: [Alice, Bob, Charlie, David, Eve]
```

    }
}
```

#### Collecting to a Map

You can collect stream elements into a map as well:

```java
import java.util.Arrays;
import java.util.List;
import java.util.Map;
import java.util.stream.Collectors;

public class CollectToMapExample {
    public static void main(String[] args) {
        List<String> names = Arrays.asList("Alice", "Bob", "Charlie",

"David");

```java
        // Collecting names into a Map where key is the name and value is the length
        Map<String, Integer> nameLengthMap = names.stream()
            .collect(Collectors.toMap(name -> name, String::length));

        System.out.println(nameLengthMap); // Output: {Alice=5, Bob=3, Charlie=7, David=5}
    }
}
```

Summary

Java Streams provide a robust API for

processing sequences of elements in a functional style. We covered the introduction to streams, stream operations such as filtering, mapping, and reducing, and how to collect data from streams into various data structures.

Streams enable a concise and expressive way to process data, making Java programming more efficient and enjoyable. As you continue to explore Java Streams, you will find that they can significantly improve code readability and reduce boilerplate code.

6. Java Input and Output: A Comprehensive Guide

Java provides a rich set of tools for handling input and output (I/O), which are essentials for proper application development. The Java I/O framework enables the reading and writing of data in a variety of formats and from different sources, including files, memory, and network connections. This guide will cover the basics of file I/O, how to read and write files, and delve into serialization in Java, complete with practical code examples.

1. File I/O Basics

In Java, file I/O is primarily handled through the classes defined in the `java.io` package. Understanding the foundational concepts is important for effective file handling.

a. Streams

At the core of Java I/O is the concept of

streams. A stream is a sequence of data that can be read from or written to. There are two main types of streams:

- **Input Streams**: Used to read data.
- **Output Streams**: Used to write data.

Streams can be byte-oriented or character-oriented:

- **Byte Streams**: Handles raw binary data. Classes like `InputStream` and `OutputStream` are its base classes.
- **Character Streams**: Handles character data (text). Classes like `Reader` and `Writer` are its base classes.

b. File Handling

To work with files in Java, we often use the `File` class, which is part of the `java.io` package. This class provides methods for creating, deleting, and checking the properties of file objects.

```java
import java.io.File;

public class FileExample {
    public static void main(String[] args) {
        File file = new File("example.txt");

        if (file.exists()) {
            System.out.println("File exists: " + file.getName());
            System.out.println("Absolute path: " + file.getAbsolutePath());
            System.out.println("Writable: " + file.canWrite());
            System.out.println("Readable: " + file.canRead());
            System.out.println("File size in bytes:
```

```
            " + file.length());
        } else {
            System.out.println("File does not exist.");
        }
    }
}
```

2. Reading and Writing Files

Java provides multiple ways to read from and write to files. We'll explore using FileReader and FileWriter for character files, as well as FileInputStream and FileOutputStream for binary files.

a. Writing Files

Using FileWriter

```java
import java.io.FileWriter;
import java.io.IOException;

public class WriteFileExample {
    public static void main(String[] args) {
        try (FileWriter writer = new FileWriter("output.txt")) {
            writer.write("Hello, World!");
            writer.write("\nThis is a test file.");
            System.out.println("File written successfully.");
        } catch (IOException e) {
            System.out.println("An error occurred while writing to the file.");
            e.printStackTrace();
        }
    }
}
```

```
}
```

Here, `FileWriter` is used to write text data to `output.txt`. The `try-with-resources` statement ensures that the `FileWriter` is closed automatically.

Using BufferedWriter

For efficiency, especially with larger data amounts, it's often recommended to use `BufferedWriter` in conjunction with `FileWriter`.

```java
import java.io.BufferedWriter;
import java.io.FileWriter;
import java.io.IOException;
```

```java
public class BufferedWriteFileExample {
    public static void main(String[] args) {
        try (BufferedWriter writer = new BufferedWriter(new FileWriter("buffered_output.txt"))) {
            writer.write("Buffered Writer Example");
            writer.newLine();
            writer.write("Writing data to a file efficiently.");
            System.out.println("Buffered file written successfully.");
        } catch (IOException e) {
            System.out.println("An error occurred while writing to the buffered file.");
            e.printStackTrace();
        }
    }
}
```

b. Reading Files

Using FileReader

Reading from a file can be accomplished similarly using `FileReader`.

```java
import java.io.FileReader;
import java.io.BufferedReader;
import java.io.IOException;

public class ReadFileExample {
    public static void main(String[] args) {
        try (BufferedReader reader = new BufferedReader(new FileReader("output.txt"))) {
            String line;
            while ((line = reader.readLine()) !=
```

```
        null) {
                System.out.println(line);
            }
        } catch (IOException e) {
            System.out.println("An error occurred while reading the file.");
            e.printStackTrace();
        }
    }
}
```

Here, `BufferedReader` is used to read lines from `output.txt` efficiently.

Using FileInputStream

If you need to read binary files, `FileInputStream` comes into play.

```java
import java.io.FileInputStream;
import java.io.IOException;

public class ReadBinaryFileExample {
    public static void main(String[] args) {
        try (FileInputStream fis = new FileInputStream("binary_file.dat")) {
            int byteData;
            while ((byteData = fis.read()) != -1) {
                System.out.print((char) byteData); // Convert byte to char for display
            }
        } catch (IOException e) {
            System.out.println("An error occurred while reading the binary file.");
            e.printStackTrace();
        }
```

    }
}
```



### 3. Serialization in Java

Serialization is the process of converting an object into a byte stream, which can then be reverted back (deserialization) into a copy of the object. This is particularly useful for saving objects to a file or sending them over a network.

#### a. Making Objects Serializable

To serialize an object, the object's class must implement the `Serializable` interface.

```java
import java.io.Serializable;

```java
public class Person implements Serializable {
    private String name;
    private int age;

    public Person(String name, int age) {
        this.name = name;
        this.age = age;
    }

    @Override
    public String toString() {
        return "Person{" + "name='" + name + '\'' + ", age=" + age + '}';
    }
}
```

b. Serializing Objects

To serialize the `Person` object, we can use `ObjectOutputStream`.

```java
import java.io.FileOutputStream;
import java.io.IOException;
import java.io.ObjectOutputStream;

public class SerializationExample {
    public static void main(String[] args) {
        Person person = new Person("Alice", 30);

        try (FileOutputStream fos = new FileOutputStream("person.ser");
             ObjectOutputStream oos = new ObjectOutputStream(fos)) {
```

```
            oos.writeObject(person);

        System.out.println("Serialization successful!");

    } catch (IOException e) {

        System.out.println("An error occurred during serialization.");

        e.printStackTrace();

        }
    }
}
```

c. Deserializing Objects

To deserialize the object, we can use `ObjectInputStream`.

```java
import java.io.FileInputStream;
```

```java
import java.io.IOException;
import java.io.ObjectInputStream;

public class DeserializationExample {
    public static void main(String[] args) {
        try (FileInputStream fis = new FileInputStream("person.ser");
             ObjectInputStream ois = new ObjectInputStream(fis)) {
            Person person = (Person) ois.readObject();
            System.out.println("Deserialized Person: " + person);
        } catch (IOException | ClassNotFoundException e) {
            System.out.println("An error occurred during deserialization.");
            e.printStackTrace();
        }
    }
}
```

```
}
```
```

```

Through this exploration, we've covered the basics of Java input and output, provided examples of reading and writing to files, and delved into the world of serialization. Java's I/O capabilities make it a powerful language for building applications that handle data efficiently.

Keep practicing these concepts to gain more fluency in Java I/O and serialization techniques, as they are essential for any Java developer working on real-world applications.

7.Multithreading and Concurrency in Java

Multithreading and concurrency are fundamental concepts in Java programming, critical for developing high-performance applications that can efficiently utilize system resources, handle multiple tasks simultaneously, and improve responsiveness. This extensive guide will explore threads, synchronization, locks, and the Executor framework, thoroughly examining their functionalities, practical examples, and real-world applications.

Understanding Threads

A **thread** is the smallest unit of execution within a process. A thread can run concurrently with other threads within the same application, allowing multiple operations to happen simultaneously. In Java, threads can be created in two main ways:

1. **By extending the Thread class**
2. **By implementing the Runnable interface**

Creating a Thread by Extending the Thread Class

When you extend the `Thread` class, you have to override the `run()` method that contains the code that will be executed when the thread starts.

Here's an example:

```java
class MyThread extends Thread {
    @Override
    public void run() {
        for (int i = 0; i < 5; i++) {
```

```java
System.out.println(Thread.currentThread().getName() + " - Count: " + i);
            try {
                Thread.sleep(100); // Sleep for 100 milliseconds
            } catch (InterruptedException e) {
                System.out.println("Thread interrupted");
            }
        }
    }
}


public class ThreadExample {
    public static void main(String[] args) {
        MyThread thread1 = new MyThread();
        MyThread thread2 = new MyThread();

        thread1.start(); // Initializes the thread
```

and calls `run()`

```
    thread2.start();
  }
}
```

Creating a Thread by Implementing the Runnable Interface

Alternatively, you can create a thread by implementing the `Runnable` interface. This is often considered a better practice as it allows for more flexibility.

Here's an example:

```java
class MyRunnable implements Runnable {
    @Override
```

```java
    public void run() {
        for (int i = 0; i < 5; i++) {
            System.out.println(Thread.currentThread().getName() + " - Count: " + i);
            try {
                Thread.sleep(100); // Sleep for 100 milliseconds
            } catch (InterruptedException e) {
                System.out.println("Thread interrupted");
            }
        }
    }
}

public class RunnableExample {
    public static void main(String[] args) {
        Thread thread1 = new Thread(new MyRunnable());
```

```
    Thread thread2 = new Thread(new MyRunnable());

    thread1.start();
    thread2.start();
  }
}
```

Thread Lifecycle

The lifecycle of a thread in Java consists of several states:

- **New**: The thread is created but not yet started.

- **Runnable**: The thread is ready to run but not necessarily executing.

- **Blocked**: The thread is waiting for a monitor lock to enter a synchronized block/method.

- **Waiting**: The thread is waiting for another thread to perform a particular action (e.g., `Object.wait()`).

- **Timed Waiting**: The thread is waiting for another thread to perform an action for up to a specified waiting time.

- **Terminated**: The thread has exited.

This lifecycle is managed by the Java Virtual Machine (JVM), which schedules thread execution based on priority and available CPU resources.

Synchronization and Locks

In a multithreaded environment, multiple threads can access shared resources concurrently, leading to potential issues such as **race conditions**, where the outcome of operations depends on the timing of the thread scheduling. To prevent this, synchronization ensures that only one thread can access a resource at a time.

Synchronized Methods and Blocks

In Java, you can synchronize methods or blocks of code. Here's how they work:

Synchronized Methods

A method can be declared with the `synchronized` keyword, preventing concurrent access.

```java
class Counter {
    private int count = 0;

    public synchronized void increment() {
        count++;
```

```java
    }

    public int getCount() {
        return count;
    }
}


public class SynchronizedMethodExample {
    public static void main(String[] args) throws InterruptedException {
        Counter counter = new Counter();
        Thread thread1 = new Thread(() -> {
            for (int i = 0; i < 1000; i++) {
                counter.increment();
            }
        });
        Thread thread2 = new Thread(() -> {
            for (int i = 0; i < 1000; i++) {
```

```
            counter.increment();
        }
    });

    thread1.start();
    thread2.start();
    thread1.join();
    thread2.join();

    System.out.println("Final Count: " + counter.getCount());
    }
}
```

Synchronized Blocks

You can also use synchronized blocks to lock only a specific portion of the code rather than the entire method, allowing for finer control over synchronization.

```java
class Counter {
    private int count = 0;

    public void increment() {
        synchronized (this) { // Lock on the current instance
            count++;
        }
    }

    public int getCount() {
        return count;
    }
}
```

Locks

Java provides more advanced locking mechanisms through the `java.util.concurrent.locks` package. The `Lock` interface offers features like try-locking and timed locks.

Here's an example using `ReentrantLock`:

```java
import java.util.concurrent.locks.Lock;
import java.util.concurrent.locks.ReentrantLock;

class LockCounter {
    private int count = 0;
    private Lock lock = new ReentrantLock();
```

```java
    public void increment() {
        lock.lock(); // Acquire the lock
        try {
            count++;
        } finally {
            lock.unlock(); // Ensure the lock is released
        }
    }

    public int getCount() {
        return count;
    }
}


public class LockExample {
    public static void main(String[] args) throws InterruptedException {
        LockCounter counter = new
```

```java
LockCounter();
    Thread thread1 = new Thread(() -> {
        for (int i = 0; i < 1000; i++) {
            counter.increment();
        }
    });
    Thread thread2 = new Thread(() -> {
        for (int i = 0; i < 1000; i++) {
            counter.increment();
        }
    });

    thread1.start();
    thread2.start();
    thread1.join();
    thread2.join();

    System.out.println("Final Count: " +
```

counter.getCount());

    }
}
```

### ReadWriteLock

When you have more read operations than write operations, you might consider using the `ReadWriteLock`, which allows multiple threads to read simultaneously but locks the resource for writing.

```java
import java.util.concurrent.locks.ReentrantReadWriteLock;

class ReadWriteCounter {
    private int count = 0;

```java
    private final ReentrantReadWriteLock lock
= new ReentrantReadWriteLock();


    public void increment() {

        lock.writeLock().lock(); // Acquire the write lock

        try {

            count++;

        } finally {

            lock.writeLock().unlock(); // Ensure the lock is released

        }
    }


    public int getCount() {

        lock.readLock().lock(); // Acquire the read lock

        try {

            return count;
```

```
        } finally {
            lock.readLock().unlock(); // Ensure the lock is released
        }
    }
}
```

Executor Framework and Concurrency Utilities

The Executor framework, introduced in Java 5, provides a higher-level replacement for managing threads. The core interface, `Executor`, is a simple interface for running asynchronous tasks, enabling better resource management and code organization.

Executor Interface

The simplest implementation of the `Executor` interface is the `ThreadPoolExecutor`, which can manage a pool of worker threads for executing submitted tasks.

Here's a basic example:

```java
import java.util.concurrent.ExecutorService;
import java.util.concurrent.Executors;

public class ExecutorExample {
    public static void main(String[] args) {
        ExecutorService executorService = Executors.newFixedThreadPool(3); // Create a thread pool with 3 threads

        for (int i = 0; i < 10; i++) {
            final int taskId = i; // Final variable for
```

the task

```
executorService.submit(() -> {
    System.out.println("Task " + taskId + " is in execution by " + Thread.currentThread().getName());
    try {
        Thread.sleep(100);
    } catch (InterruptedException e) {
        Thread.currentThread().interrupt();
    }
});
      }

      executorService.shutdown(); // Shutdown the executor
   }
}
```

Callable and Future

For tasks that return a value, you can use the `Callable` interface and receive the result through a `Future`.

```java
import java.util.concurrent.Callable;
import java.util.concurrent.ExecutionException;
import java.util.concurrent.ExecutorService;
import java.util.concurrent.Executors;
import java.util.concurrent.Future;

public class CallableExample {
    public static void main(String[] args) throws ExecutionException, InterruptedException {

        ExecutorService executorService = Executors.newFixedThreadPool(2);
```

```
        Callable<Integer> task = () -> {
            Thread.sleep(1000); // Simulate long running task
            return 123; // Return a result
        };


        Future<Integer> future = executorService.submit(task);
        System.out.println("Task submitted. Waiting for result...");
        System.out.println("Result: " + future.get()); // Blocks until the result is available

        executorService.shutdown();
    }
}
```

Fork/Join Framework

For dividing a larger problem into smaller tasks, the Fork/Join framework is available. You can fork tasks recursively and then join the results, which is excellent for parallel processing.

```java
import java.util.concurrent.RecursiveTask;
import java.util.concurrent.ForkJoinPool;

class SumTask extends RecursiveTask<Integer> {
    private final int start;
    private final int end;

    public SumTask(int start, int end) {
        this.start = start;
        this.end = end;
```

```java
    }


    @Override
    protected Integer compute() {
        if (end - start <= 10) { // Threshold for task division
            int sum = 0;
            for (int i = start; i <= end; i++) {
                sum += i;
            }
            return sum;
        }


        int mid = (start + end) / 2;
        SumTask leftTask = new SumTask(start, mid);
        SumTask rightTask = new SumTask(mid + 1, end);
```

```java
        leftTask.fork(); // Fork the left task

        int rightResult = rightTask.compute(); // Compute the right task

        int leftResult = leftTask.join(); // Join the left task result


        return leftResult + rightResult; // Combine the results
    }
}


public class ForkJoinExample {
    public static void main(String[] args) {
        ForkJoinPool pool = new ForkJoinPool();
        SumTask task = new SumTask(1, 100);
        int result = pool.invoke(task); // Start the ForkJoin process


        System.out.println("Sum: " + result); //
```

Output the result

   }

}

```

### Concurrency Utilities

Java also provides various concurrency utility classes in the `java.util.concurrent` package, including:

- **CountDownLatch**: A synchronization aid that allows one or more threads to wait until a set of operations in other threads completes.

- **CyclicBarrier**: A synchronization barrier that allows a set of threads to wait for each other to reach a common barrier point.

- **Semaphore**: A counting semaphore that can be used to control access to a particular resource.
```

Here is an example of using `CountDownLatch`:

```java
import java.util.concurrent.CountDownLatch;

public class CountDownLatchExample {
    public static void main(String[] args) throws InterruptedException {
        CountDownLatch latch = new CountDownLatch(3); // Create a CountDownLatch for 3 threads

        for (int i = 0; i < 3; i++) {
            final int id = i + 1;
            new Thread(() -> {
                System.out.println("Thread " + id + " is working...");
                try {
                    Thread.sleep((long)
```

```
            (Math.random() * 1000));
                } catch (InterruptedException e) {
                    e.printStackTrace();
                }
                latch.countDown(); // Count down when the thread completes
                System.out.println("Thread " + id + " completed.");
            }).start();
        }

        latch.await(); // Wait until all threads have completed
        System.out.println("All threads have completed.");
    }
}
```

Multithreading and concurrency in Java provide a powerful way to build efficient, responsive applications. Understanding threads, synchronization methods and locks, and leveraging the Executor framework and various concurrency utilities allows developers to harness the full capabilities of modern multi-core processors. By implementing these concepts with care, you can achieve optimal performance and manage complexity in your Java applications. Remember, however, that with great power comes great responsibility—the proper handling of concurrent processing is critical, as improper implementations can lead to bugs that are hard to diagnose.

Thus, mastering these technologies is key to any serious Java programmer, particularly those involved in systems programming, web applications, and enterprise-level applications that require robust, high-performance solutions.

8. Java GUI Programming

Graphical User Interfaces (GUIs) are essential for creating user-friendly applications. Java provides powerful libraries such as Swing and AWT (Abstract Window Toolkit) to develop rich desktop applications. In this chapter, we will explore the fundamentals of GUI programming in Java, focusing on the following sections:

- Introduction to Swing and AWT

- Creating Basic GUI Applications

- Event Handling in Java

Introduction to Swing and AWT

AWT (Abstract Window Toolkit)

AWT is the original Java GUI toolkit that facilitates the creation of user interfaces in

Java applications. It is built on the operating system's native components, making it platform-dependent in behavior and appearance. AWT provides a set of graphical components such as buttons, text fields, checkboxes, and other graphical objects.

Example of AWT:

```java
import java.awt.*;
import java.awt.event.*;

public class AWTExample {
    public static void main(String[] args) {
        Frame frame = new Frame("AWT Example");
        Button button = new Button("Click Me");
```

```java
        button.setBounds(30, 100, 80, 30);
        frame.add(button);

        frame.setSize(300, 300);
        frame.setLayout(null);
        frame.setVisible(true);

        frame.addWindowListener(new WindowAdapter() {
            public void windowClosing(WindowEvent we) {
                System.exit(0);
            }
        });
    }
}
```

Swing

Swing is a more advanced GUI toolkit introduced in Java to overcome the limitations of AWT. It provides a richer set of components and does not rely on the native desktop system's widgets. Swing components are lightweight, meaning they are written entirely in Java, which allows for greater flexibility and customizability. Swing is part of the `javax.swing` package and supports features like pluggable look-and-feel, which allows developers to change the appearance of UI components easily.

Key Features of Swing:

- Pluggable Look and Feel: You can change the appearance of your GUI components easily.

- Lightweight: Swing components are rendered by Java, not by the operating system.

- Richer Components: Swing provides advanced components like trees, tables, and text areas.

Example of a Simple Swing Application:

```java
import javax.swing.*;
import java.awt.event.*;

public class SwingExample {
    public static void main(String[] args) {
        JFrame frame = new JFrame("Swing Example");
        JButton button = new JButton("Click Me");

        button.setBounds(50, 100, 95, 30);
        frame.add(button);

        frame.setSize(400, 400);
        frame.setLayout(null);
        frame.setVisible(true);
```

```
frame.setDefaultCloseOperation(JFrame.EXIT_ON_CLOSE);

        button.addActionListener(new ActionListener() {
            public void actionPerformed(ActionEvent e) {
                JOptionPane.showMessageDialog(frame, "Button Clicked!");
            }
        });
    }
}
```

Creating Basic GUI Applications

Creating a basic GUI application in Java involves several steps, including setting up the main frame, adding components (like buttons, text fields, labels), and setting the layout.

Step 1: Create the Main Frame

The primary component of a GUI application is the main window (or frame). With Swing, this is typically done with a `JFrame`.

Step 2: Adding Components

You can add various GUI components like buttons, text fields, and labels to the frame. These components can be arranged using different layout managers provided by the Swing toolkit.

Step 3: Setting Layouts

Layouts determine the arrangement of components within containers. Common layouts in Swing include FlowLayout, GridLayout, BorderLayout, and BoxLayout.

Example of a Basic Calculator Using Swing:

```java
import javax.swing.*;
import java.awt.*;
import java.awt.event.*;

public class Calculator extends JFrame implements ActionListener {
    // Creating GUI Components
    JTextField inputField;
    JButton[] numberButtons;
    JButton addButton, subButton, mulButton, divButton, equButton, clrButton;
```

```java
double num1, num2, result;
char operator;

public Calculator() {
    // Frame settings
    setTitle("Calculator");
    setSize(400, 500);
    setLayout(null);

    inputField = new JTextField();
    inputField.setBounds(30, 40, 340, 40);
    add(inputField);

    numberButtons = new JButton[10];
    for (int i = 0; i < 10; i++) {

        numberButtons[i] = new JButton(String.valueOf(i));

        numberButtons[i].setBounds(30 + (i % 3) * 100, 100 + (i / 3) * 60, 80, 50);
```

```java
numberButtons[i].addActionListener(this);
    add(numberButtons[i]);
}


// Arithmetic buttons
addButton = new JButton("+");
addButton.setBounds(330, 100, 50, 50);
addButton.addActionListener(this);
add(addButton);


subButton = new JButton("-");
subButton.setBounds(330, 160, 50, 50);
subButton.addActionListener(this);
add(subButton);


mulButton = new JButton("*");
mulButton.setBounds(330, 220, 50, 50);
```

```java
mulButton.addActionListener(this);
add(mulButton);


divButton = new JButton("/");
divButton.setBounds(330, 280, 50, 50);
divButton.addActionListener(this);
add(divButton);


equButton = new JButton("=");
equButton.setBounds(30, 340, 250, 50);
equButton.addActionListener(this);
add(equButton);


clrButton = new JButton("C");
clrButton.setBounds(300, 340, 50, 50);
clrButton.addActionListener(this);
add(clrButton);
```

```java
        setVisible(true);

setDefaultCloseOperation(EXIT_ON_CLOSE);
    }


    public void actionPerformed(ActionEvent e) {
        for (int i = 0; i < 10; i++) {
            if (e.getSource() == numberButtons[i]) {

inputField.setText(inputField.getText().concat(String.valueOf(i)));
            }
        }
        if (e.getSource() == addButton) {
            num1 = Double.parseDouble(inputField.getText());
            operator = '+';
```

```java
        inputField.setText("");
    }
    if (e.getSource() == subButton) {
        num1 = Double.parseDouble(inputField.getText());
        operator = '-';
        inputField.setText("");
    }
    if (e.getSource() == mulButton) {
        num1 = Double.parseDouble(inputField.getText());
        operator = '*';
        inputField.setText("");
    }
    if (e.getSource() == divButton) {
        num1 = Double.parseDouble(inputField.getText());
        operator = '/';
        inputField.setText("");
```

```java
        }
    if (e.getSource() == equButton) {
        num2 = Double.parseDouble(inputField.getText());
        switch (operator) {
            case '+':
                result = num1 + num2;
                break;
            case '-':
                result = num1 - num2;
                break;
            case '*':
                result = num1 * num2;
                break;
            case '/':
                result = num1 / num2;
                break;
        }
```

```
        inputField.setText(String.valueOf(result));
    }
    if (e.getSource() == clrButton) {
        inputField.setText("");
        num1 = num2 = 0;
    }
  }


  public static void main(String[] args) {
    new Calculator();
  }
}
```

Explanation of the Calculator Application:

1. **Frame Creation:**

- We create a `JFrame` to hold our calculator GUI.

- The frame size is set, and the layout is defined as `null` to use absolute positioning.

2. **Input Field:**

- A `JTextField` is used to display the input and result.

3. **Number Buttons:**

- We create an array of `JButton` for digits 0-9, arranged on the frame using calculated bounds.

4. **Arithmetic Buttons:**

- Each arithmetic operation (addition, subtraction, multiplication, division) has its own button.

5. **Action Handling:**

- The `actionPerformed` method handles button clicks, performing calculations and updating the input field accordingly.

Event Handling in Java

Event handling is an integral part of GUI programming and allows the application to respond to user actions such as clicks, key presses, and mouse movements. In Java, event handling is primarily accomplished through the use of listener interfaces.

Common Listener Interfaces:

1. **ActionListener**: Used for button clicks and menu selections.

2. **MouseListener**: Handles mouse events like clicks and movements.

3. **KeyListener**: Handles keyboard events.

4. **WindowListener**: Monitors changes in window states (opening, closing, resizing, etc.).

Example of ActionListener:

Let's expand our previous example by adding an additional button and using `ActionListener` to manage its actions:

```java
import javax.swing.*;
import java.awt.event.*;

public class ButtonEventExample extends JFrame implements ActionListener {
    JButton helloButton, exitButton;

    public ButtonEventExample() {
        setTitle("Button Event Example");
```

```java
setSize(300, 200);
setLayout(null);

helloButton = new JButton("Say Hello");
helloButton.setBounds(30, 50, 120, 30);
helloButton.addActionListener(this);
add(helloButton);

exitButton = new JButton("Exit");
exitButton.setBounds(160, 50, 80, 30);
exitButton.addActionListener(this);
add(exitButton);

setVisible(true);

setDefaultCloseOperation(EXIT_ON_CLOSE);
}
```

```java
    public void actionPerformed(ActionEvent e) {
        if (e.getSource() == helloButton) {
            JOptionPane.showMessageDialog(this, "Hello World!");
        }
        if (e.getSource() == exitButton) {
            System.exit(0);
        }
    }

    public static void main(String[] args) {
        new ButtonEventExample();
    }
}
```

Explanation of ButtonEventExample:

1. **Frame Creation**: Similar to previous examples, we create the main window and set its properties.

2. **Buttons**:
   - `helloButton` displays a greeting message.
   - `exitButton` closes the application.

3. **actionPerformed**: The listener determines which button was clicked and executes the appropriate action, either displaying a message dialog or exiting the program.

KeyListener Example:

You can also handle keyboard events using `KeyListener`. Here's a simple program that responds to key presses:

```java
```

```java
import javax.swing.*;
import java.awt.event.*;

public class KeyListenerExample extends JFrame implements KeyListener {
    JTextField textField;

    public KeyListenerExample() {
        setTitle("Key Listener Example");
        setSize(400, 200);
        setLayout(null);

        textField = new JTextField();
        textField.setBounds(50, 50, 300, 30);
        add(textField);
        textField.addKeyListener(this);

        setVisible(true);
```

```java
        setDefaultCloseOperation(EXIT_ON_CLOSE);
    }

    public void keyTyped(KeyEvent e) {
        // Handle key typed event
        System.out.println("Key Typed: " + e.getKeyChar());
    }

    public void keyPressed(KeyEvent e) {
        // Handle key pressed event
        System.out.println("Key Pressed: " + e.getKeyCode());
    }

    public void keyReleased(KeyEvent e) {
        // Handle key released event
```

```
        System.out.println("Key Released: " + e.getKeyCode());

    }

    public static void main(String[] args) {

        new KeyListenerExample();

    }
}
```

Explanation of KeyListenerExample:

1. **KeyListener Implementation**: We implement `KeyListener` and override three methods to handle typing, pressing, and releasing keys.

2. **Text Field**: Adding a text field where keys can be typed allows us to capture keyboard events.

3. **Event Handling**: Each key event prints the character or key code to the console, demonstrating how to capture and respond to user keyboard input.

Java GUI programming, mainly using Swing and AWT, provides developers with the tools to create powerful and interactive desktop applications. By mastering the concepts of components, layouts, and event handling, developers can create a wide variety of applications that are both functional and user-friendly.

In this overview, we covered the introduction to GUI toolkits, foundational application design, and important event handling techniques in Java. With this knowledge, you can begin developing your own Java GUI applications, exploring further examples, and refining your skills in GUI design and event-driven programming.

9. Networking in Java

Networking is a crucial aspect of modern software development, enabling applications to communicate and share data over the internet or local networks. Java, being a platform-independent language, provides a robust set of libraries and APIs for networking. In this article, we will explore the concepts of Java networking, discuss working with sockets, and build a simple client-server application.

Understanding Java Networking

Java provides a rich set of APIs for network programming, particularly in the `java.net` package. This package contains classes for implementing both low-level and high-level networking operations.

Key Concepts

1. **IP Address**: In networking, each device on the internet is identified by a unique IP address. This can be an IPv4 address (like 192.168.1.1) or an IPv6 address (like 2001:0db8:85a3:0000:0000:8a2e:0370:7334).

2. **Port**: A port is a communication endpoint that allows multiple services to run on a single IP address. Ports are identified by numbers, ranging from 0 to 65535. Standard applications like HTTP (80) and HTTPS (443) have well-known ports.

3. **Protocols**: Network protocols determine how data is transmitted over the network. The most common ones are TCP (Transmission Control Protocol) and UDP (User Datagram Protocol).

Java Networking Classes

1. **Socket**: This class represents a socket that can be used for client-server

communication.

2. **ServerSocket**: This class is used to create a server that listens for incoming client connections.

3. **InetAddress**: This class represents an IP address and provides methods to resolve hostnames.

4. **URL**: This class represents a Uniform Resource Locator, which is used to access resources on the internet.

5. **URLConnection**: This class is used to create a connection to a URL and read data from it.

Working with Sockets

What is a Socket?

A socket is one endpoint in a two-way communication link between two programs running on the network. The `Socket` class in Java provides methods to connect to a server, send and receive data, and close the connection.

Creating a Socket

To create a socket in Java, you typically provide the IP address and the port number of the server you wish to connect to. Here's an example of creating a socket:

```java
import java.io.*;
import java.net.*;

public class SimpleClient {
    public static void main(String[] args) {
```

```java
        String serverAddress = "localhost";
        int port = 1234;


    try {
        // Create a socket to connect to the server
        Socket socket = new Socket(serverAddress, port);

        // Output stream to send data to the server
        PrintWriter out = new PrintWriter(socket.getOutputStream(), true);

        // Input stream to receive data from the server
        BufferedReader in = new BufferedReader(new InputStreamReader(socket.getInputStream()));
```

```java
            // Send a message to the server
            out.println("Hello Server!");

            // Read response from server
            String response = in.readLine();
            System.out.println("Server Response: " + response);

            // Close the streams and the socket
            in.close();
            out.close();
            socket.close();
        } catch (IOException e) {
            e.printStackTrace();
        }
    }
}
```
```
```

Explanation

- We import necessary packages and create the `SimpleClient` class.

- We specify the server address and port.

- We create a `Socket` object to connect to the server.

- We create output and input streams to send and receive messages.

- We send a greeting to the server and wait for a response.

Building a Simple Client-Server Application

Now that we understand how to work with sockets, let's build a simple client-server application. The server will listen for incoming connections, and the clients will send messages to get a response.

Step 1: Create the Server

Here's a simple implementation of a server that listens on a specified port and responds to client messages:

```java
import java.io.*;
import java.net.*;

public class SimpleServer {
    public static void main(String[] args) {
        int port = 1234;

        try {
            // Create a ServerSocket to listen on the specified port
            ServerSocket serverSocket = new
```

```java
ServerSocket(port);
System.out.println("Server is listening on port " + port);

while (true) {
    // Accept an incoming client connection
    Socket socket = serverSocket.accept();
    System.out.println("New client connected");

    // Create input and output streams for the client
    BufferedReader in = new BufferedReader(new InputStreamReader(socket.getInputStream()));
    PrintWriter out = new PrintWriter(socket.getOutputStream(), true);

    // Read the message from the client
```

```java
            String clientMessage = in.readLine();
            System.out.println("Received: " + clientMessage);

            // Send a response back to the client
            out.println("Hello Client! You said: " + clientMessage);

            // Close the resources
            in.close();
            out.close();
            socket.close();
        }
    } catch (IOException e) {
        e.printStackTrace();
    }
  }
}
```

```

### Explanation

- The server listens for incoming connections on port `1234`.

- When a client connects, it creates input and output streams for communication.

- The server reads the client's message and sends a response.

- Finally, the server closes the resources after handling the client.

### Step 2: Create the Client

We have already created a client in the previous section, but here's a refined version for the sake of completeness:

```java

```java
import java.io.*;
import java.net.*;

public class SimpleClient {
    public static void main(String[] args) {
        String serverAddress = "localhost";
        int port = 1234;

        try {
            // Create a socket to connect to the server
            Socket socket = new Socket(serverAddress, port);

            PrintWriter out = new PrintWriter(socket.getOutputStream(), true);

            BufferedReader in = new BufferedReader(new InputStreamReader(socket.getInputStream()));

            // Send a message to the server
```

```
            out.println("Hello Server!");

            // Read response from server
            String response = in.readLine();
            System.out.println("Server Response: " + response);

            // Close the streams and the socket
            in.close();
            out.close();
            socket.close();
        } catch (IOException e) {
            e.printStackTrace();
        }
    }
}
```

Step 3: Running the Application

1. **Start the Server**: First, compile and run the `SimpleServer` class. It will listen for connections.

2. **Run the Client**: Compile and run the `SimpleClient` class. It will connect to the server, send a message, and display the server's response.

Step 4: Testing Multiple Clients

To see how the server handles multiple clients, you can run multiple instances of the `SimpleClient` application. Each will connect to the server and send messages, while the server responds to each one.

Conclusion

In this article, we explored networking in

Java, focusing on sockets and client-server communication. We built a simple client-server application that sends and receives messages. Java's networking capabilities offer a solid foundation for building more complex applications, such as web servers, chat applications, online gaming, and more.

Further Enhancements

1. **Multi-threading**: You might want to enhance the server to handle multiple clients simultaneously using threads. Each time a client connects, a new thread can be spawned to handle that connection.

2. **Error Handling**: More robust error handling mechanisms can be implemented to manage different types of exceptions.

3. **Data Formats**: Consider using serialization or JSON to format data being transmitted between client and server for more

complex applications.

4. **Security**: For production applications, consider implementing security measures such as SSL for secure communication.

5. **Scalability**: Explore using frameworks like Java RMI or libraries that facilitate RESTful interactions.

Networking in Java is powerful and versatile, enabling developers to create a wide range of networked applications efficiently.

10. Java Web Development: An In-Depth Overview

Introduction to Servlets and JSP

Java web development predominantly revolves around servlets and JavaServer Pages (JSP). These technologies allow developers to create dynamic web content powered by the Java programming language, enabling robust web applications.

Servlets: The Backbone of Java Web Applications

What are Servlets?

Servlets are Java classes that handle requests and responses in a web application. They run on a web server and function as a middle layer between client requests and data responses, providing dynamic content generation.

Lifecycle of a Servlet

1. **Loading**: The servlet container loads the servlet class into memory.

2. **Instantiating**: It creates an instance of the servlet.

3. **Initialization**: The servlet's `init()` method is called, allowing for any initialization parameters.

4. **Request Handling**: Each time a request is received, the servlet's `service()` method is invoked, handling requests through `doGet()` or `doPost()` methods depending on the request type.

5. **Destruction**: When the servlet is no longer needed, the `destroy()` method is called, allowing cleanup operations.

Example of a Simple Servlet

Here's an example of a basic servlet that responds to a user's request:

```java
import java.io.IOException;
import java.io.PrintWriter;
import javax.servlet.ServletException;
import javax.servlet.annotation.WebServlet;
import javax.servlet.http.HttpServlet;
import javax.servlet.http.HttpServletRequest;
import javax.servlet.http.HttpServletResponse;

@WebServlet("/hello")
public class HelloServlet extends HttpServlet {
    protected void doGet(HttpServletRequest request, HttpServletResponse response)
            throws ServletException, IOException {
        response.setContentType("text/html");
        PrintWriter out = response.getWriter();
```

```
        out.println("<html><body>");
        out.println("<h1>Hello, World!</h1>");
        out.println("</body></html>");
    }
}
```

To deploy this servlet, you would typically package it in a WAR file and configure your web server (such as Apache Tomcat) to recognize it at the specified endpoint (`/hello`).

JavaServer Pages (JSP)

What is JSP?

JavaServer Pages (JSP) simplifies the process of creating dynamic content. Unlike servlets, JSP allows developers to embed Java code directly into HTML pages. It compiles into a servlet by the container, providing a seamless integration between HTML and Java code.

Example of a Simple JSP Page

Here's a simple example of a JSP file:

```jsp
<%@ page language="java" contentType="text/html; charset=UTF-8"
    pageEncoding="UTF-8"%>
<%@ taglib uri="http://java.sun.com/jsp/jstl/core" prefix="c" %>
<html>
<head>
    <title>Welcome JSP Page</title>
</head>
<body>
```

```
    <h1>Welcome to JSP!</h1>

    <p>Current Date and Time: <%= new java.util.Date() %></p>
</body>
</html>
```

In this example, we use `<%= ... %>` to insert Java code directly into the HTML, producing dynamic content seamlessly without the verbosity of full servlets.

Building a Simple Web Application

To understand how these technologies work in tandem, let's build a simple web application that allows users to enter their names and see a greeting.

Application Structure

1. **Project Setup**: We will use Apache Tomcat as our server.

2. **Directory Structure**:

```
WebApp/
├── WEB-INF/
│   ├── web.xml
│   └── classes/
├── index.jsp
└── greet.jsp
```

Step 1: Create the `web.xml` Deployment Descriptor

In `WEB-INF/web.xml`, we define our servlet and its mapping:

```xml
```

```xml
<web-app xmlns="http://xmlns.jcp.org/xml/ns/javaee"

xmlns:xsi="http://www.w3.org/2001/XMLSchema-instance"

xsi:schemaLocation="http://xmlns.jcp.org/xml/ns/javaee
    http://xmlns.jcp.org/xml/ns/javaee/web-app_3_1.xsd"
    version="3.1">
  <servlet>
    <servlet-name>GreetServlet</servlet-name>
    <servlet-class>GreetServlet</servlet-class>
  </servlet>
  <servlet-mapping>
    <servlet-name>GreetServlet</servlet-name>
    <url-pattern>/greet</url-pattern>
```

```
    </servlet-mapping>
</web-app>
```

Step 2: Create the `GreetServlet`

Next, we create a servlet that reads the user's name from the request and forwards it to a JSP page:

```java
import java.io.IOException;
import javax.servlet.ServletException;
import javax.servlet.annotation.WebServlet;
import javax.servlet.http.HttpServlet;
import javax.servlet.http.HttpServletRequest;
import javax.servlet.http.HttpServletResponse;
```

```java
@WebServlet("/greet")
public class GreetServlet extends HttpServlet {

    protected void doPost(HttpServletRequest request, HttpServletResponse response)
            throws ServletException, IOException {

        String name = request.getParameter("name");
        request.setAttribute("userName", name);

        request.getRequestDispatcher("greet.jsp").forward(request, response);
    }
}
```

Step 3: Create `index.jsp`

This is the entry point of our application

where users can enter their names:

```jsp
<%@ page contentType="text/html;charset=UTF-8" language="java" %>
<html>
<head>
    <title>Greeting App</title>
</head>
<body>
    <h1>Enter your name</h1>
    <form action="greet" method="post">
        Name: <input type="text" name="name" required />
        <input type="submit" value="Greet Me!" />
    </form>
</body>
```

</html>
```

### Step 4: Create `greet.jsp`

Finally, the JSP page that displays the greeting:

```jsp
<%@ page language="java" contentType="text/html; charset=UTF-8"
    pageEncoding="UTF-8"%>
<html>
<head>
    <title>Greeting</title>
</head>
<body>
    <h1>Hello, <%= request.getAttribute("userName") %>!</h1>

```
            <a href="index.jsp">Go back</a>
    </body>
</html>
```

Conclusion of the Simple Web Application

You can now deploy this application on Tomcat. When users access `index.jsp`, they can enter their name, submit the form, and be greeted on the `greet.jsp` page. This simple application illustrates how servlets and JSP work together in Java web development.

Overview of Spring Framework

The Spring Framework is a comprehensive framework for Java applications, known for its ability to simplify enterprise Java development. It offers extensive infrastructure support, making it easier to build complex applications.

Core Features of Spring

1. **Dependency Injection (DI)**: Spring promotes loose coupling through the DI design pattern, allowing for greater testability and maintainability.

2. **Aspect-Oriented Programming (AOP)**: It enables the separation of cross-cutting concerns such as logging and transaction management from business logic.

3. **Spring MVC**: A powerful web framework that provides a model-view-controller architecture for building web applications.

4. **Data Access**: Simplifies database access via JDBC and JPA integration.

Spring MVC Architecture

The architecture consists of three main components:

- **Model**: Represents the data and the business logic.
- **View**: The presentation layer that represents the model in a user-friendly format.
- **Controller**: Handles user requests, interacts with the model, and determines the response.

Example of a Simple Spring MVC Application

To illustrate Spring MVC, let's create a simple application similar to the earlier one:

Project Structure

```
```

```
SpringWebApp/
├── src/main/java/com/example/
│   ├── controller/
│   │   └── GreetingController.java
│   ├── model/
│   │   └── Greeting.java
├── src/main/resources/
│   └── application.properties
├── src/main/webapp/
│   ├── WEB-INF/
│   │   └── web.xml
│   └── index.jsp
└── pom.xml
```

Step 1: Dependency Management with Maven

Your `pom.xml` should include dependencies for Spring and JSP:

```xml
<dependencies>
  <dependency>
    <groupId>org.springframework</groupId>
    <artifactId>spring-webmvc</artifactId>
    <version>5.3.9</version>
  </dependency>
  <dependency>
    <groupId>javax.servlet</groupId>
    <artifactId>javax.servlet-api</artifactId>
    <version>4.0.1</version>
    <scope>provided</scope>
  </dependency>
  <dependency>
    <groupId>javax.servlet.jsp</groupId>
```

```
        <artifactId>javax.servlet.jsp-api</artifactId>
        <version>2.0.0</version>
        <scope>provided</scope>
    </dependency>
</dependencies>
```

Step 2: Create the Model Class

The model represents the greeting in our application:

```java
package com.example.model;

public class Greeting {
    private String name;
```

```java
    public Greeting(String name) {
        this.name = name;
    }

    public String getName() {
        return name;
    }
}
```

Step 3: Create the Controller Class

The controller will handle HTTP requests:

```java
package com.example.controller;

import com.example.model.Greeting;
```

```java
import org.springframework.stereotype.Controller;
import org.springframework.ui.Model;
import org.springframework.web.bind.annotation.PostMapping;
import org.springframework.web.bind.annotation.RequestMapping;


@Controller
public class GreetingController {

    @RequestMapping("/")
    public String index() {
        return "index";
    }

    @PostMapping("/greet")
    public String greet(String name, Model
```

```
    model) {
        Greeting greeting = new Greeting(name);
        model.addAttribute("greeting", greeting);
        return "greet";
    }
}
```

Step 4: Create the `web.xml`

The deployment descriptor for your Spring MVC application:

```xml
<web-app xmlns="http://xmlns.jcp.org/xml/ns/javaee"

xmlns:xsi="http://www.w3.org/2001/XMLSchema-instance"
```

```xml
    xsi:schemaLocation="http://xmlns.jcp.org/xml/ns/javaee
        http://xmlns.jcp.org/xml/ns/javaee/web-app_3_1.xsd"
        version="3.1">
    <servlet>
        <servlet-name>dispatcher</servlet-name>
        <servlet-class>org.springframework.web.servlet.DispatcherServlet</servlet-class>
        <load-on-startup>1</load-on-startup>
    </servlet>
    <servlet-mapping>
        <servlet-name>dispatcher</servlet-name>
        <url-pattern>/</url-pattern>
    </servlet-mapping>
</web-app>
```

```

#### Step 5: Create the JSP Pages

- **index.jsp**:

```jsp
<%@ page contentType="text/html;charset=UTF-8" language="java" %>
<html>
<head>
    <title>Greeting App</title>
</head>
<body>
    <h1>Enter your name</h1>
    <form action="/greet" method="post">
        Name: <input type="text" name="name" required />

```
    <input type="submit" value="Greet Me!" />
  </form>
</body>
</html>
```

- **greet.jsp**:

```jsp
<%@ page contentType="text/html; charset=UTF-8"
    pageEncoding="UTF-8"%>
<html>
<head>
    <title>Greeting</title>
</head>
<body>
    <h1>Hello, ${greeting.name}!</h1>
```

```html
    <a href="/">Go back</a>
</body>
</html>
```

Conclusion of the Spring MVC Application

This application captures user input through a form and greets the user dynamically using Spring MVC. By leveraging Spring's architecture, we can enhance scalability, maintainability, and separation of concerns.

Final Thoughts

Java web development has transformed over the years, from simple servlets and JSP to advanced frameworks like Spring that facilitate the creation of more complex applications. As web technology continues to evolve, the principles of good design and robust architecture remain critical for developers seeking to build high-quality, maintainable web applications. Whether you're snowballing with servlets or soaring with Spring, Java web development offers powerful tools for creating dynamic, enterprise-level applications.

11. Testing in Java

Testing is a critical aspect of software development that ensures the quality and reliability of applications. In the Java programming ecosystem, various methodologies and tools are employed to facilitate effective testing. This article will explore several testing paradigms, including Unit Testing using JUnit, Test-Driven Development (TDD), and Mocking with Mockito. It will also delve into best practices and design patterns necessary for code quality and maintainability, along with common design patterns in Java and useful refactoring techniques.

Unit Testing with JUnit

What is Unit Testing?

Unit testing is the process of testing individual components or "units" of code to verify that they function as expected. In Java, the most widely used framework for unit testing is JUnit. JUnit provides a simple but powerful way to write and execute tests, allowing developers to isolate code and ensure correctness.

Getting Started with JUnit

To begin using JUnit, you need to include the JUnit library in your Java project. If you're using Maven, you can add the following dependency to your `pom.xml` file:

```xml
<dependency>
    <groupId>junit</groupId>
    <artifactId>junit</artifactId>
    <version>4.13.2</version>
    <scope>test</scope>
</dependency>
```

```

### Writing Your First Test

Here's a simple example to illustrate how unit tests are structured using JUnit. Assume we have a class `Calculator` with a method that adds two integers:

```java
public class Calculator {
    public int add(int a, int b) {
        return a + b;
    }
}
```

Now, let's create a unit test for this `add` method using JUnit:
```

```java
import static org.junit.Assert.assertEquals;
import org.junit.Test;

public class CalculatorTest {

    private Calculator calculator = new Calculator();

    @Test
    public void testAdd() {
        int result = calculator.add(2, 3);
        assertEquals(5, result);
    }
}
```

In this example, the `assertEquals` method checks whether the expected result (5) matches the actual result returned by the `add` method. If they do not match, the test will fail.

Running JUnit Tests

JUnit tests can be run directly within an IDE like IntelliJ or Eclipse, or from the command line using Maven or Gradle. Running tests automatically helps to catch regressions and bugs early in the development process.

Test-Driven Development (TDD)

What is TDD?

Test-Driven Development is a software development process that relies on a short, iterative cycle of writing tests before writing the corresponding code. The TDD cycle comprises three primary steps:

1. **Red**: Write a failing test that defines a desired improvement or new function.

2. **Green**: Write the minimum amount of code necessary to make the test pass.

3. **Refactor**: Clean up the newly added code while ensuring that all tests still pass.

TDD Example

Let's illustrate TDD with the `Calculator` class. Suppose we start by wanting to add a method to subtract two numbers.

1. **Red**: First, we write a test for the subtract method, which doesn't exist yet.

```java
@Test
public void testSubtract() {
    int result = calculator.subtract(5, 3);
```

```
    assertEquals(2, result);
}
```

When we run this test, it will fail because the `subtract` method doesn't exist.

2. **Green**: Next, implement the `subtract` method in the `Calculator` class:

```java
public int subtract(int a, int b) {
    return a - b;
}
```

Now, when you run the tests, the `testSubtract` method should pass.

3. **Refactor**: If necessary, make any code improvements while keeping an eye on ensuring all tests continue to pass.

This approach encourages you to think about the design and requirements of your class upfront, leading to a better-structured codebase.

Mocking with Mockito

What is Mocking?

Mocking is a technique used in unit testing to simulate the behavior of complex objects. This is especially important when dealing with dependencies that are not easy to control or are external, such as databases, web services, or other APIs.

Getting Started with Mockito

To use Mockito, include the following dependency in your `pom.xml`:

```xml
<dependency>
    <groupId>org.mockito</groupId>
    <artifactId>mockito-core</artifactId>
    <version>3.11.2</version>
    <scope>test</scope>
</dependency>
```

Using Mockito

Consider a scenario in which the `Calculator` depends on a `Logger` class to log operations. Here's a simplified version of the classes:

```java
```

```java
public class Logger {
    public void log(String message) {
        System.out.println(message);
    }
}


public class Calculator {
    private Logger logger;

    public Calculator(Logger logger) {
        this.logger = logger;
    }

    public int add(int a, int b) {
        int result = a + b;
        logger.log("Adding: " + result);
        return result;
    }
```

```
    }
```

Now, we want to test the `Calculator` class without actually printing to the console. Here's how to mock the `Logger` using Mockito:

```java
import static org.mockito.Mockito.*;
import org.junit.Test;

public class CalculatorTest {

    @Test
    public void testAddLogsCorrectly() {
        Logger loggerMock = mock(Logger.class);
        Calculator calculator = new Calculator(loggerMock);
```

```
        calculator.add(2, 3);


        verify(loggerMock).log("Adding: 5");
    }
}
```

In this test, we create a mock of the `Logger` class and verify that the `log` method is called with the correct message when the `add` method is executed.

Best Practices and Design Patterns

Code Quality and Maintainability

Ensuring high code quality and maintainability is essential for long-term success in software development. Here are some best practices:

1. **Consistent Naming Conventions**: Use clear and consistent naming for classes, methods, and variables. Names should reflect the purpose of the element.

2. **Small Classes and Methods**: Aim for small, focused classes and methods. Each class should have a single responsibility, in line with the Single Responsibility Principle (SRP).

3. **Comment and Document**: Although self-explanatory code is ideal, adding comments and documentation can significantly enhance code readability.

4. **Use Code Review**: Implement code review practices to catch issues early and promote knowledge sharing among team members.

5. **Automate Testing**: Integrate automated tests into your development workflow to catch regressions and ensure software quality.

Common Design Patterns in Java

Design patterns are proven solutions to recurring design problems in software development. Here are a few common design patterns in Java:

1. **Singleton Pattern**: Ensures a class has only one instance and provides a global point of access to it.

```java
public class Singleton {

    private static Singleton instance;

    private Singleton() {}
```

```java
    public static Singleton getInstance() {
        if (instance == null) {
            instance = new Singleton();
        }
        return instance;
    }
}
```

2. **Factory Pattern**: Provides an interface for creating objects in a superclass but allows subclasses to alter the type of objects that will be created.

```java
public abstract class Shape {
    public abstract void draw();
}
```

```java
public class Circle extends Shape {
    @Override
    public void draw() {
        System.out.println("Drawing a circle");
    }
}


public class Square extends Shape {
    @Override
    public void draw() {
        System.out.println("Drawing a square");
    }
}


public class ShapeFactory {
    public static Shape getShape(String shapeType) {
        if (shapeType.equalsIgnoreCase("CIRCLE")) {
```

```java
        return new Circle();
    } else if (shapeType.equalsIgnoreCase("SQUARE")) {
        return new Square();
    }
    return null;
  }
}
```

3. **Decorator Pattern**: Allows behavior to be added to individual objects, either statically or dynamically, without affecting the behavior of other objects from the same class.

```java
public interface Coffee {
    String getDescription();
    double cost();
```

```java
}


public class SimpleCoffee implements Coffee {

    @Override
    public String getDescription() {
        return "Simple Coffee";
    }

    @Override
    public double cost() {
        return 1.00;
    }
}


public abstract class CoffeeDecorator implements Coffee {
    protected Coffee decoratedCoffee;
```

```java
    public CoffeeDecorator(Coffee decoratedCoffee) {

        this.decoratedCoffee = decoratedCoffee;

    }


    public String getDescription() {

        return decoratedCoffee.getDescription();

    }


    public double cost() {

        return decoratedCoffee.cost();

    }

}


public class MilkDecorator extends CoffeeDecorator {

    public MilkDecorator(Coffee decoratedCoffee) {

        super(decoratedCoffee);
```

```
    }


    @Override

    public String getDescription() {

        return decoratedCoffee.getDescription() + ", Milk";

    }


    @Override

    public double cost() {

        return decoratedCoffee.cost() + 0.50;

    }
}
```

Refactoring Techniques

Refactoring is the process of restructuring existing code without changing its external behavior. Here are some useful refactoring techniques:

1. **Extract Method**: If a method is too long or complex, consider breaking it into smaller methods that encapsulate individual behaviors.

2. **Replace Magic Numbers with Constants**: Using constants instead of hard-coded numbers improves code readability and maintainability.

3. **Inline Method**: If a method is not doing enough to warrant its existence, consider replacing calls to that method with the method's content.

4. **Introduce Parameter Object**: When a method has too many parameters, consider creating a new class (parameter object) to group these parameters together.

5. **Split Variable**: If a variable is used for multiple purposes, consider splitting it into separate variables, each serving a single purpose.

Testing in Java is integral to developing high-quality software applications. Methods such as Unit Testing with JUnit, Test-Driven Development, and Mocking with Mockito provide powerful approaches to ensure code correctness and reliability. Alongside effective testing practices, adhering to best practices in code quality and utilizing common design patterns significantly contributes to the maintainability and scalability of Java applications. Moreover, employing strategic refactoring techniques helps evolve the codebase while keeping it clean and efficient. By combining these practices, developers can build robust, maintainable, and testable software systems confidently.

12. Java Syntax and Glossary

Java is one of the most widely used programming languages across the globe. It was developed by Sun Microsystems in the mid-'90s and has since evolved significantly. Java is an object-oriented, high-level programming language that is designed to be platform-independent at both the source and binary levels. To fully understand Java, one must grasp its syntax, keywords, and core concepts. This document aims to provide a comprehensive overview of Java syntax, accompanied by a glossary of key terms related to the language.

Java Syntax

1. Basic Structure of a Java Program

Java programs consist of a series of classes. Each class contains methods that define what the program does. The basic structure of a

Java program can be illustrated as follows:

```java
class ClassName {
    // Method declaration
    returnType methodName(parameters) {
        // Method body
    }

    public static void main(String[] args) {
        // Entry point of the program
    }
}
```

2. Comments

Comments are essential for documenting your

code and are ignored by the compiler. Java supports three types of comments:

- **Single-line comments** start with `//`.
- **Multi-line comments** are enclosed between `/*` and `*/`.
- **Documentation comments** start with `/**` and can be used to generate external documentation tools like Javadoc.

Example:

```java
// This is a single-line comment

/*
This is a multi-line comment
*/
```

```
/**
 * This is a documentation comment
 */
```

3. Data Types

Java is a statically typed language, meaning all variables must be declared with a data type. The main data types include:

- **Primitive Data Types:**
    - `int` (integer)
    - `double` (floating point)
    - `char` (character)
    - `boolean` (true/false)

- **Reference Data Types:** Used for classes, arrays, or interfaces.

Example:

```java
int number = 10;
double price = 20.99;
char letter = 'A';
boolean isJavaFun = true;
```

4. Variables

A variable in Java is a container that holds data that can change during the execution of a program. Variable declarations involve specifying the data type followed by the variable name.

Example:

```java
```

```
String name = "Alice";
int age = 25;
```

5. Operators

Java supports various operators, including:

- **Arithmetic Operators:** `+`, `-`, `*`, `/`, `%`
- **Relational Operators:** `==`, `!=`, `>`, `<`, `>=`, `<=`
- **Logical Operators:** `&&`, `||`, `!`
- **Assignment Operators:** `=`, `+=`, `-=`, `*=`, `/=`

Example:
```java
int sum = 5 + 10; // Arithmetic
```

```
boolean result = (5 < 10) && (10 > 5); // Logical
```

6. Control Statements

Control statements direct the flow of the program. They can include:

- **Conditional Statements:** `if`, `else`, `switch`
- **Loop Statements:** `for`, `while`, `do-while`

Example of an `if` statement:
```java
if (age >= 18) {
    System.out.println("You are an adult.");
} else {
```

    System.out.println("You are a minor.");
}
```


Example of a `for` loop:
```java
for (int i = 0; i < 5; i++) {
    System.out.println("Iteration: " + i);
}
```


7. Arrays

Arrays are collections of similar data types. In Java, arrays are objects, and their size is fixed once defined.

Example:
```java

```java
int[] numbers = {1, 2, 3, 4, 5};

System.out.println(numbers[0]); // Accessing the first element
```

8. Methods

Methods are blocks of code that perform specific tasks and can be called upon multiple times. They can return values and accept parameters.

Example:
```java
public int add(int a, int b) {
    return a + b;
}
```

9. Classes and Objects

Java is an object-oriented programming (OOP) language, and it supports the creation of classes and objects. A class serves as a blueprint for objects, containing attributes (fields) and methods.

Example:
```java
class Car {
    String color;
    int year;

    void displayInfo() {
        System.out.println("Color: " + color + ", Year: " + year);
    }
}
```

```
// Creating an object
Car myCar = new Car();
myCar.color = "Red";
myCar.year = 2020;
myCar.displayInfo();
```

10. Inheritance

Inheritance allows one class to inherit fields and methods from another. The keyword `extends` is used to establish inheritance.

Example:
```java
class Vehicle {
    void sound() {
        System.out.println("Vehicle sound");
    }
```

```
    }

    class Bike extends Vehicle {
        void sound() {
            System.out.println("Bike sound");
        }
    }
```

11. Interfaces

An interface in Java is a reference type, similar to a class, that can contain only constants, method signatures, default methods, static methods, and nested types. Interfaces cannot contain instance fields and are abstract by default.

Example:

```java
```

```java
interface Vehicle {
    void start();
    void stop();
}
```

12. Exception Handling

Java provides a robust exception handling mechanism to manage runtime errors. The keywords `try`, `catch`, and `finally` are used for exception handling.

Example:

```java
try {
    int result = 10 / 0; // This will cause an exception
} catch (ArithmeticException e) {
```

```
    System.out.println("Division by zero is not allowed.");

} finally {

    System.out.println("This block executes regardless of an exception.");

}
```

Glossary of Java Terms

- **Java Virtual Machine (JVM):** An engine that provides runtime environment to execute Java bytecode. It converts bytecode into machine language.

- **Java Development Kit (JDK):** A software development environment used to develop Java applications. It contains the JRE, tools, and libraries.

- **Java Runtime Environment (JRE):** A

part of the JDK that provides libraries, Java Virtual Machine (JVM), and other components to run applications written in Java.

- **Bytecode:** The compiled Java code that the JVM interprets.

- **Object:** An instance of a class that contains state (fields) and behavior (methods).

- **Class:** A blueprint or prototype for creating objects. It encapsulates data for the object.

- **Method:** A block of code that performs a specific task; methods are invoked or called to execute their code.

- **Encapsulation:** The bundling of data (attributes) and methods that operate on data within one unit or class; it restricts direct access to some of an object's components.

- **Abstraction:** The concept of hiding the complex reality while exposing only the necessary parts; it helps to reduce programming complexity.

- **Polymorphism:** The ability of a variable, function, or object to take on multiple forms; it allows methods to perform differently based on the object that it acts upon.

- **Inheritance:** A mechanism wherein a new class is derived from an existing class, inheriting fields and methods from the parent class.

- **Interface:** A reference type in Java, similar to a class, that can contain only constants, method signatures, default methods, static methods, and nested types.

- **Constructor:** A special method invoked when an object is instantiated. It is mainly used to initialize fields of the object.

- **Garbage Collection:** The automatic process by which Java manages memory. The JVM automatically frees up memory by deleting objects that are no longer in use.

- **API (Application Programming Interface):** A set of routines, protocols, and tools for building software and applications.

- **Framework:** A set of libraries or classes that provides a foundation for building applications. Examples include Spring and Hibernate.

- **Thread:** A lightweight subprocess, the smallest unit of processing that can be executed concurrently with other threads.

- **Synchronization:** A mechanism that ensures that two or more concurrent processes do not simultaneously execute critical sections of code, often used to prevent data inconsistency.

- **JavaBeans:** A reusable software component that follows specific conventions, such as having a no-argument constructor.

- **Annotation:** A form of metadata that provides data about a program but is not part of the program itself. Annotations have no direct effect on the code but can direct a compiler, a framework, or whatever the runtime uses.

Java is a robust programming language with a rich syntax and extensive vocabulary. Understanding Java's basic syntax, data types, control structures, and object-oriented programming principles is essential for any developer working in the Java ecosystem. The glossary provided is a helpful resource for familiarizing oneself with the terminology used in Java. Mastering these concepts will empower developers to write efficient, maintainable, and scalable Java applications.

Index

1. Introduction pg.4

2. Java Basics pg.17

3. Object-Oriented Programming in Java pg.36

4. Java Collections Framework pg.59

5. Working with Java Streams pg.79

6. Java Input and Output: A Comprehensive Guide pg.94

7. Multithreading and Concurrency in Java pg.110

8. Java GUI Programming pg.138

9. Networking in Java pg.164

10. Java Web Development: An In-Depth Overview pg.180

11. Testing in Java pg. 206

12. Java Syntax and Glossary pg.228

www.ingramcontent.com/pod-product-compliance
Lightning Source LLC
Chambersburg PA
CBHW052145220526
45471CB00004B/1533